Young Pathfinder 7

Making the link

Relating languages to other work i...

Other titles in the Young Pathfinder series

A flying start! Introducing early language learning (YPF11)
Peter Satchwell and June de Silva

A world of languages: Developing children's love of languages (YPF10)
Manjula Datta and Cathy Pomphrey

The literacy link (YPF9)
Catherine Cheater and Anne Farren

Grammar is fun (YPF8)
Lydia Biriotti

Let's join in! Rhymes, poems and songs (YPF6)
Cynthia Martin and Catherine Cheater

First steps to reading and writing (YPF5)
Christina Skarbek

Keep talking: Teaching in the target language (YPF4)
Peter Satchwell

Are you sitting comfortably?: Telling stories to young language learners (YPF3)
Daniel Tierney and Patricia Dobson

Games and fun activities (YPF2)
Cynthia Martin

CILT, the National Centre for Languages, seeks to support and develop multilingualism and intercultural competence among all sectors of the population in the UK.

CILT serves education, business and the wider community with:
- specialised and impartial information services;
- high quality advice and professional development;
- expert support for innovation and development;
- quality improvement in language skills and service provision.

CILT is a charitable trust, supported by the DfES and other Government departments throughout the UK.

ELL is a DfES initiative managed by CILT, the National Centre for Languages, working in partnership with QCA, BECTA, the British Council Education and Training Group, the TTA, OFSTED and the Association for Language Learning.

Young Pathfinder 7

A CILT series for primary language teachers

Making the link

Relating languages to other work in the school

*Daniel Tierney
and Malcolm Hope*

The views expressed in this book are those of the authors and do not necessarily represent the views of CILT.

Acknowledgements

The Scottish Office for permission to reproduce examples from the training programme.

The Consejería de Educación for permission to reproduce the cover of *El pueblo do Lola*.

Hobkirk PS for the model House. Mike Donaghy and Mary Yarr of the Education and Library Board, Armagh, for permission to use the Easter illustration.

All the primary language teachers who have inspired and helped with this publication.

First published 1998
by the Centre for Information on Language Teaching and Research (CILT)
20 Bedfordbury, London, WC2N 4LB.

Copyright © Centre for Information on Language Teaching and Research 1998

ISBN 1 902031 04 0

A catalogue record for this book is available from the British Library.

All rights reserved. No part of this publication may be reproduced, stored in a retrieval system, or transmitted in any form or by any means, electronic, mechanical, photocopying, recording, or otherwise, without the prior permission in writing from CILT or under licence from the Copyright Licensing Agency Limited, of 90 Tottenham Court Road, London W1T 4LP.

The right of Daniel Tierney and Malcolm Hope to be identified as authors of this work has been asserted by them in accordance with the Copyright, Designs and Patents Act, 1988.

Printed in the United Kingdom by Hobbs the Printers Ltd, Totton, Hampshire SO40 3WX

CILT Publications are available from: **Central Books**, 99 Wallis Rd, London E9 5LN. Tel: 0845 458 9910. Fax: 0845 458 9912. Book trade representation (UK and Ireland): **Broadcast Book Services**, Charter House, 27a London Rd, Croydon CR0 2RE. Tel: 020 8681 8949. Fax: 020 8688 0615.

Contents

	Page
Contents	
Introduction	1
Linking to other areas of the curriculum	2
Teaching aspects of the curriculum itself	3
1 Around the school	5
The physical environment	5
Everyday contact	5
Classroom language	6
2 The village theme	8
Inventing the village	8
The inhabitants	9
A different type of village?	10
3 Other common themes	12
Healthy living	12
Survey	12
Games	13
Cooking	13
Stories and songs	15
The European Union	17
The countries	17
The flags	18
Currency	18
Music	20
Houses	21
The rooms and furniture	21
The inhabitants	22
Other themes	23
The book as the theme	23

4 Festivals 24
   Christmas 24
      Making things 24
      Songs and carols 28
      Storytelling 29
   Other festivals 29
      Easter 29
      Halloween/Shrovetide 31

5 Linking the foreign language to curriculum subjects 34
   Mathematics 34
      Surveys 34
      Shapes 35
   English (knowledge about language) 35
      Dictionary skills 36
   Geography 36
   Design and technology 37
   Physical education 40
   Music 41
   Drama 41

6 Extending the link — and the learner 42
   Mathematics 43
      Activities 44
   Physical Education 52
      Jeux d'échauffement (warm-up games) 53
      Main activities 54
      Parachute games 57

Conclusion 58

Useful sources 59

Introduction

One of the first decisions a primary school embarking on teaching a modern language has to make is which approach to adopt. There are perhaps two essential questions:

DO WE WISH TO RAISE PUPILS' GENERAL AWARENESS OF LANGUAGE?

By exposing them to one or more foreign languages, they can appreciate that languages often have words which look and sound the same as, or similar to, words in their own language, and they discover some of the reasons why. They learn that other languages sometimes use completely different sounds to those in our own language. They begin to understand that languages are governed by rules, and that these rules are sometimes similar and sometimes different in various languages. They become aware that when languages are written down, families of languages use the same script, and that some languages link script to sound quite closely, while others (such as English) do not. For some linguists, 'educating the ear' of young children and enabling them to develop mimicry of different sounds is a prime reason for an early start to language learning, and the ability to recall, speak and write with meaningful accuracy are secondary aims.

DO WE WISH TO DEVELOP THE PUPILS' SKILLS IN A SPECIFIC LANGUAGE?

By giving time on the timetable to a subject called 'German', do we expect a defined and measurable competence in listening, speaking, reading and writing of German by the time pupils leave primary school?

In a nutshell, do we want to teach them **about** language or teach them a **particular** language?

Within the United Kingdom in recent years, most primary language projects have opted to follow the second approach and to try and extend the period of learning a language.

However, that then raises three further questions:

- To what extent is the language to be seen as a timetabled and separate subject?
- To what extent can we link the children's language experience to the other work going on in the classroom and school?
- To what extent can we actually teach aspects of the primary curriculum through the medium of the foreign language?

There are times when the programme for part or all of Modern Languages in the Primary School (MLPS) may be taught as a separate subject and for a variety of good reasons. There is no right or wrong approach.

However, this book explores the latter two of the three questions above and deals with links between the foreign language and other subjects.

 LINKING TO OTHER AREAS OF THE CURRICULUM

The reasons for doing so may include:

- a desire to reinforce concepts already developed through other related work in English language, mathematics, environmental studies or expressive arts;

- a wish to exploit wall displays created as part of a theme. To take the example of a class that had been studying the European Union and, as part of their art work, had produced a tremendous display of European countries' flags. This offered a magnificent resource for exploiting work on colours, nationalities and countries which were part of the agreed cluster programme. This example is developed further in Chapter 3;

- wanting to save on some curricular time by relating the MLPS work to part of other work which would normally have been conducted in English;

- working to the strengths of teachers who have some competence in a foreign language but are not extensively trained to teach it. They may welcome the security of teaching familiar material in familiar ways, rather than to have to learn and apply a wholly new methodology.

In Scotland a national training programme in French, German, Italian and Spanish has been devised for primary teachers. Many of the ideas and examples in Chapters 1–5 have come from the Scottish primary project which first started with a pilot in 1989 and is now being extended to every primary school in Scotland.

In these chapters the teacher will find ways in which the language can be related to other areas of the curriculum without actually teaching the curriculum itself. The primary language teacher may wish to consider this approach as a first step. Many of the ideas are simple and easy to use, making a little language go a long way. They are suitable for pupils in the final years of primary school. Most of the examples have been developed through French, but there are also some from other languages.

Thus, if the primary teacher is considering developing a theme such as health, he or she may go to Chapter 3 for ideas on how to relate language work to that theme. If it is Christmas time, he or she will find ideas in Chapter 4 so that the foreign language finds a natural place.

The more confident linguist, however, may wish to go more quickly to the following approach.

 TEACHING ASPECTS OF THE CURRICULUM ITSELF

The reasons for adopting this approach may include:

- the saving of curricular time, as there is obviously no need for a separate slot in the timetable. For colleagues in England and Wales who need to audit their subject time, the MFL time comes from (and can be double-counted as) subject time, i.e. when a science activity is done through French, this is 'science time' in the audit;

- the purposeful and real nature of the language experience. When there is a known and clear context in which the language is used, it is easier to understand it;

- a teacher whose foreign language competence is adequate though not expert may feel more secure in teaching the foreign language through familiar subjects and topics where assurance and expertise already exist;

- pupils have a chance to 'acquire' as well as 'learn' language. Linguists often stress the difference between, on the one hand, acquisition through immersion in the language to the point where it is absorbed without conscious effort, e.g. by immigrant workers in a community or children plunged into a school where their mother tongue is not spoken and, on the other hand, learning through planned, structured and progressive teaching;

- a programme of study which regards acquisition rather than the defined-content learning of particular structures and vocabulary of a foreign language as the goal is much less likely to pose continuity problems when pupils transfer to secondary schools.

In Chapter 6 the teacher will find ways of moving towards actually teaching aspects of the curriculum itself. These are based on a collection of materials produced for an in-service training course for primary teachers of French in Oxfordshire. The activities link directly to Key Stage 2 and show how aspects of the curriculum at that stage may be recycled and re-experienced by the pupils through the medium of French, in this instance.

Whichever of the two approaches is used — or when to use both — will depend on a number of factors such as:

- the confidence and competence of the teacher;
- the aims and objectives of your primary language programme;
- the nature of what you are doing elsewhere in the curriculum.

It is hoped that in the following chapters you will find lots of ideas to bring the language alive, to set it in meaningful contexts and to make the link . . .

1. Around the school

One of the most effective ways to link the foreign language to other areas is for it to find its place in the normal routine and life of the school. Peter Satchwell in *Keep talking (YPF4)* looks at many aspects and provides useful lists of phrases which can be used throughout the day. We do not wish to duplicate that work but to look instead at the general principles of linking the language to the work of the class.

THE PHYSICAL ENVIRONMENT

The best place to start would probably be at the school entrance. One Scottish Primary visited had two cardboard figures at the door with the banner '*Bienvenidos a St Blane's*' (Welcome to St Blane's).

Once through the door, primary school corridors often make it clear that this is a French or Italian or Spanish or German school.

Walls are covered with friezes of their French village (see Chapter 2), the story of *The very hungry caterpillar* in German, the project work in Italy, the healthy eating message in Spanish.

In some schools the janitor's room, the office, the staff room, etc are labelled by the children in the foreign language.

EVERYDAY CONTACT

In one three-class village primary school the German teacher conducted a small part of assembly in German for the whole school. This could include such things as greetings, offering praise to particular classes or pupils, offering birthday congratulations to pupils whose birthday was that day or week. Singing *Happy birthday* every day is to be avoided! It could also include a prayer or hymn, if appropriate, or a song or a Christmas carol. The idea is to bring the language into the normal life of the school and to encourage a positive attitude among the pupils, rather than develop their linguistic competence as such.

It is generally the case that only some classes (mostly the older pupils) are learning the language. However, some colleagues can usually be persuaded to extend the language experience. Thus the five-year-olds may be used to greetings in French, the six-year-olds may have, in addition, the register being conducted in French and the seven-year-olds may have both those activities and the organising of lunches in French. The school secretary may be willing to join in by also using French for greetings, farewells and asking how the children are. In one school visited the children enjoyed using *Buenos días Señor McNeil* (Good morning . . .) and *Hasta luego/adios Señor McNeil* (Goodbye) with the school caretaker who responded in Spanish.

CLASSROOM LANGUAGE

Within the actual class there are many commonly encountered classroom situations and these are developed fully for use with the target language in *Keep talking (YPF4)*. Thus an older class may have been used to seeing the language around the school and perhaps hearing it at assembly. They may have been exposed to basic language in their earlier classes and now they can be told in the foreign language to line up, to hang up their coats and to enter the classroom quietly. Once there, all the daily routine of register, lunches, changing the date and weather chart, is done in the target language. In some schools it may be appropriate to start the day with a prayer (see opposite). Perhaps PE exercises or a little mental arithmetic could also be used to start the day (see Chapter 5).

Before lunchtime or at the end of the day the pupils could be dismissed in the foreign language. This may be done in simple expressions or could involve language such as *'tous les garçons qui ont les cheveux noirs', 'toutes les filles qui portent une jupe grise'* (all the boys with black hair, all the girls who are wearing a grey skirt).

All of this is using language for a real purpose and for normal activities which would have been happening anyway. The language is linked to the daily life of the school even before we consider the actual language lesson itself.

Prayers

Morgengebet

Danke für Sonne, Mond und Sterne,
Danke für Wald und Feld und Berge,
Danke für alle deine Tiere,
Danke für jedes Volk der Erde.

Danke für Wiese, Meer und Täler,
Danke für Wolken, Wind und Regen,
Danke für alle deine Vögel,
Danke für deine Lieb' und Segen.

Das Vaterunser

Unser Vater im Himmel!
Geheiligt werde dein Name.
Dein Reich komme.
Dein Wille geschehe
wie im Himmel, so auf Erden.
Unser tägliches Brot gib uns heute.
Und vergib uns unsere Schuld,
wie auch wir vergeben unseren Schuldigern.
Und führe uns nicht in Versuchung,
sondern erlöse uns von dem Bösen.
Amen.

Zwei Tischgebete

Segne, Vater, diese Speise,
uns zur Kraft und dir zum Preise. Amen.

Komm, Herr Jesu, sei unser Gast,
und segne, was du uns bescheret hast.
Amen.

Padre nuestro

Padre nuestro que estás en los cielos, santificado sea tu nombre, venga a nosotros tu Reino, hágase tu voluntad así en la tierra como en el cielo.

Danos hoy el pan de cada día y perdona nuestras ofensas, como nosotros perdonamos a los que nos ofenden, no nos dejes caer en la tentación y líbranos de todo mal. Amén.

(El pan nuestro de cada día dánosle hoy y perdona nuestras deudas así como nosotros perdonamos a nuestros deudores y no nos dejes caer en la tentación mas líbranos del mal. Amén.)

Ave Maria

Dios te salve María,
llena eres de gracia,
el Señor es contigo,
bendita tú eres entre todas
las mujeres y bendito
es el fruto de tu vientre
Jesús.
Santa María, Madre de Dios,
ruega por nosotros pecadores
ahora y en la hora de
nuestra muerte. Amén.

Je vous salue Marie

Je vous salue Marie, pleine de grâce,
le Seigneur est avec vous.
Vous êtes bénie entre toutes les femmes,
et Jésus, le fruit de vos entrailles est béni.
Sainte Marie, Mère de Dieu, priez pour nous,
pauvres pécheurs, maintenant et à l'heure de
notre mort. Amen.

2. The village theme

One of the most common links in Scottish primaries has been to use the village as a theme, a topic which is commonly studied. Looking at a village, perhaps the children's own village, can lead them to work in English, in maths, in geography, in art and craft/design and technology and many other subjects. These are developed through the theme of the village.

> **The Area Around My Village**
>
> My Village is situated in the French Alps. The mountains are to the east and west of the village. A line of cable cars run from the village to the mountains. To the north of my village there is a river which runs into a lake. There is a forest which surrounds the north side of my lake.
>
> In the summer my lake would be used for water sports such as water skiing and swimming. My forest would be used for picnic's. In the winter the mountains would be good for skiing. There are chalets, hotels, houses and many shops for you to buy sovenier's. A small police station and a doctor's office. There are lots of places of amusement such as a disco, sports centre, picnic area and cafes. There is a bank, Post Office and supermarket.

Learning aims & objectives

To use the village theme as a vehicle for developing the foreign language.

The following topic areas may be covered:
- *points of the compass and other locations;*
- *people and descriptive language;*
- *buildings in the village.*

INVENTING THE VILLAGE

The first stage is to invent the village, to give it a name. The children look at a map of the country and choose some names of existing towns/villages. These names, written on the board, can then be used to develop an understanding of the sound patterns. A poll is then taken to establish the class preference — *qui préfère . . . ?* Alternatively, the pupils can invent similar names before again deciding on the class preference.

Then where is the village to be? Is it to be in the North, South, East or West? Is it to be in the mountains, by the sea, near a lake? When deciding this, the teacher can revise concepts such as points of the compass, and also introduce that new language. Features such as mountains can be taught using visuals — flashcards, photographs or perhaps a symbol which can later be placed on a village frieze. It may be the case that the pupils have already completed a frieze of a village as part of their earlier study in English and that this offers a rich visual resource for the foreign language work.

The village also has buildings — a hall, a baker's, a café, a church. The children can decide if there is (. . .) in our village. *Est-ce qu'il y a (. . .) dans notre village?* If the frieze has been done beforehand, you have ready made visual aids to teach the vocabulary for shops, buildings, etc. If not, then the creation of these can be done as part of their art work and added to the developing wall frieze.

Adding to the frieze can also lead to language work for a real purpose, such as practising prepositions. You may ask the pupils where something is located. Here? There? Left? Right? *Où est situé le . . ? Ici? Là? A gauche? A droite?* Situating shops as well as geographical features could also be planned by using co-ordinates. A grid is created with 1–10 along the top and the letters A–J down the side. Colours are used, e.g. brown to represent mountains, blue for water, etc and the picture is gradually built up. Alternatively, symbols could be used. This activity also provides an opportunity for work with numbers and the alphabet.

THE INHABITANTS

We now have our village. We know where it is, its name and what's in it. A village needs to have people and their children and pets.

The people of the village need to be invented. They have to have their identities created — their names, their ages, their physical characteristics, their dates of birth. A lot of language work flows from the natural context of the village.

The pupils can each take on the identity of one of the villagers and create a pen picture of that person, perhaps on the word processor. There are also the pets and the common animals which can be taught at this stage. Motivation for learning is higher as the pupils see a reason — these pets are going to form part of their storyline.

Il cane

Il cane della famiglia si chiama Bruno. Ha tre anni. É grande e docile. É un dalmata, bianco con macchie nere.

Young Pathfinder 7: *Making the link* — 9

The next stage in creating the village will be to decide on the jobs which the people do. Thus we have M. Dupont *le boulanger* (the baker); Mme Picard *la fermière* (the farmer); M. Perrotel *le facteur* (the postman); Mme Duval *la dentiste* (the dentist); Mlle Durand *la chanteuse* (the singer), etc.

A DIFFERENT TYPE OF VILLAGE?

These are the basic details usually required for the village. However, pupils may wish to create a bizarre village. All the buildings could be painted differently: *une église verte* (a green church); *une poste rouge* (a red post office) and so on. *Notre est un peu bizarre. De quelle couleur est notre église/poste?* (Our is a little strange. What colour is our church/post office?) This offers lots of work on colours and perhaps other adjectives as well as lots of enjoyment. Pupils' imaginations can also go wild with visitors to the village from outerspace. Their Martians can have four legs, three arms, two heads, each with one eye, etc. The teacher can offer the class different possibilities as he or she creates the visitor(s): *Il a une tête ronde ou ovale?* (Does he have a round or oval head?) — teaching/reinforcing shapes; *Il a deux, trois ou quatre bras?* (Does he have two, three or four arms?) — teaching/reinforcing numbers and parts of the body; *Le bras droit est jaune ou bleu?* (Is his right arm yellow or blue?) — teaching/reinforcing right, left, colours and parts of the body.

Obviously, the village theme can also lend itself to other language work, e.g. giving directions around the village using a large floor plan; looking in detail at the interior of a house; going shopping at the village market. The whole context of the village offers an exciting way of developing many areas of language.

If you are a teacher of Spanish, you might like to look at a wonderful pack, *El pueblo de Lola*, available from the Consejería de Educación y Ciencia, Embajada de España, 20 Peel Street, London W8 7PD.

VOCABULARY

Locating the village

au nord	in the north	*au sud*	in the south
à l'est	in the east	*à l'ouest*	in the west
à la montagne	in the mountains	*près de la mer*	near the sea

Some village buildings

le café	cafe	*le marché*	market
la boulangerie	baker's	*la patisserie*	cake shop
la boucherie	butcher's	*la pharmacie*	chemist
l'église	church	*l'épicerie*	grocer's

Some inhabitants

le curé	priest	*le fermier*	farmer
le facteur	postman	*le médecin*	doctor
le boulanger	baker	*le dentiste*	dentist
l'instituteur	teacher	*en retraite*	retired

A different village

Le monstre — comment est-il ?	What is the monster like ?
Il a combien de têtes?	How many heads does it have ?
Il a combien de nez ?	How many noses does it have ?
pieds ?	How many feet does it have ?
bras ?	How many arms does it have ?
Il a une tête ronde ou ovale ?	Does he have a round or oval head ?
Le bras gauche est de quelle couleur ?	What colour is his left arm ?

3. Other common themes

The village is undoubtedly the most common theme to date in Scottish primary schools. However, as experience has been gained, other themes have emerged which also provide a rich context for language work.

 ## HEALTHY LIVING

Health education is obviously an important aspect of the curriculum. The pupils are involved in English language work: reading, speaking and writing about what is healthy. They are involved in mathematical work relating to weight, calories, etc and carrying out surveys. They are involved in art work creating a wall frieze showing which foods are healthy and which are not. Where can the foreign language fit in?

Obviously, the wall frieze or pictures can provide a visual stimulus for the basic teaching of the vocabulary. However, we want to go beyond merely learning a list of nouns.

Learning aims & objectives

To use the theme of healthy living as a vehicle for developing the foreign language.

The following topic areas may be covered:
- *food and drink;*
- *likes and dislikes;*
- *parts of the body.*

SURVEY

Ask your pupils to find out what their classmates eat and record the results on a chart.

Have a large chart on the wall with a visual representation of some healthy foods — fruits, vegetables — and some unhealthy foods — crisps, cakes — and ask the whole class who has eaten these items the day before/that week, e.g. *Qui a mangé les oranges hier/cette semaine?* Stick a coloured square on the chart for each child who answers 'yes' for the particular item of food. As you do so, ask the children to count. By the end of this process there is a complete bar graph showing the eating habits of the whole class. You can draw together the results — *Combien d'élèves ont mangé . . ?* (How many have eaten . . ?)

The pupils can also carry out a similar type of activity in groups to collate their results, produce and present their graphs. To do so, they need a limited amount of language in addition to the basic vocabulary and will be manipulating a simple past tense for a real purpose (see vocabulary on p15).

GAMES

Assemble the pupils and identify three areas of the class or gym: one representing healthy, one unhealthy, the third 'OK'. These areas can be represented by a coloured circle, e.g. green for go (healthy), red for stop (unhealthy) and amber for neither particularly healthy nor unhealthy. Use pictures/flashcards which you keep hidden from the pupils. Looking at each flashcard, ask the pupils to decide if that item is good for their health, bad for their health or in the neutral category and to walk/run to that area. Once they have decided, show the card and attach it to that area of the classroom saying, e.g.:

It is healthy to eat . . .
C'est bon pour la santé de manger . . .
Ça vous fait du bien de manger . . .

This can also be played as a boardgame. Using a basic snakes and ladders board, combined with a set of picture cards of the basic food items, the pupils can practise counting and social language, as well as the new vocabulary and expressions. Each child takes it in turn to throw the die and count out the numbers as he or she moves the counter. If it lands on a square with a ladder, the player turns over a picture card. If it is a healthy item, he or she says the expression practised above, *c'est bon pour la santé,* and goes up the ladder. If it is not, he or she stays put. In the case of a snake, if a pupil turns over a picture of *un gâteau,* he or she says it is bad for one's health, *c'est mauvais pour la santé,* and goes down the snake. If he or she turns over e.g., *les carottes,* he or she would stay put.

COOKING

The children can be involved in listen and do activities making things such as salad rolls or a fresh fruit salad.

The fruit salad features in the Scottish training programme for primary French teachers and is a common activity in Scottish classrooms.

The pupils are shown ingredients first of all the. Ask them to repeat each item as you do so.

> Il faut:
> Des bananes
> Des pommes
> Des oranges
> Des fraises
> Des raisins
> Du jus d'orange
> Un bol
> Une cuillère

The pupils are then taken through a set of easy to follow steps:

> Lavez-vous les mains.
> Epluchez les pommes/
> les oranges/les bananes.
> Coupez les . . .
> Mettez les . . . dans le bol.
> Ajoutez du jus d'orange.
> Mélangez les fruits.

The instructions for the activity can lead onto other language activities. Symbols representing each stage are drawn onto card and the corresponding text printed onto other cards. These cards can then be used to play pelmanism. The same text cards provide the pupils with a sequencing task.

Taken from the Staff Development CD-i reproduced with thanks to the Scottish Interactive Technology Centre.

Little pieces of food can be mixed together on a plate, e.g. a strawberry, a grape, a piece of orange and a little chocolate and the children involved in a blindfolded tasting game. Ask them to try and identify the food items and comment on whether they are healthy or unhealthy.

STORIES AND SONGS

The story *The very hungry caterpillar* by Eric Carle (Picture Puffin Series) deals with a lot of food. Work on that story can be combined with the theme of healthy eating. The additional expressions *C'est bon pour la santé* (It is good for your health) and *C'est mauvais pour la santé* (It is bad for your health) could be incorporated into the story or developed after the story itself. The story could be adapted and amended to *The very hungry **and healthy** caterpillar*, with the substitution of new food items for those which are bad for your health.

There is a common storyline used in Scottish schools. It is the story of Billy Hughes, a young boy who is lazy, does no exercise and eats all the wrong things. It is used for a variety of areas of the curriculum and Spanish has been added, as can be seen on p16.

There are also a number of songs which could link to the theme of health. These include *Tête, épaules, genoux et pieds, Savez-vous planter les choux?* and *Avec mon panier*. Cynthia Martin and Catherine Cheater provide more ideas for songs and rhymes in *Let's join in (YPF6)*.

VOCABULARY

Food

les oranges	oranges	*les fraises*	strawberries
les pommes	apples	*les bananes*	bananas
les raisins	grapes	*les poires*	pears
les carottes	carrots	*les tomates*	tomatoes
la salade	lettuce	*les légumes*	vegetables
les gateaux	cakes	*les bonbons*	sweets
le chocolat	chocolate	*les frites*	chips

Drink

de l'eau	water	*du lait*	milk	*du coca*	coke
de la limonade	lemonade	*du café*	coffee	*du thé*	tea

Survey

Qui a mangé les oranges hier/cette semaine?	Who ate oranges yesterday/ this week?
Combien d'élèves ont mangé . . ?	How many have eaten . . ?
Qui a mangé . . ?	Who has eaten . . ?
Tu as mangé . . ?	Have you eaten . . ?
x élèves ont mangé . . .	x pupils have eaten . . .

Commenting

C'est bon pour la santé de manger . . .	It is healthy to eat . . .
Ça vous fait du bien de manger . . .	It is good for you to eat . . .
C'est mauvais pour la santé	It is bad for your health

UNIT STUDY: Health Topic — Billy Hughes

ART/CRAFT Large picture of Billy Collage of Billy's daily food intake Dream scene (race sequence) Large pictures of wasteground scenes Small frieze of smoky living-room scene Pictures/postcards for anti-smoking campaign Collages of healthy foods **MATHS** **Pie graphs** 1 Billy's day 2 Children's own daily routine 3 Billy's new routine **Graphs** Favourite foods, hobbies, etc (Use of computer)	**DRAMA** Role play — playground discussions Conversations between Billy and his mother **SCIENCE/HEALTH** Worksheets on body parts (in Spanish) Health hazards of rubbish dumps Looking at all structures Healthy eating Anti-smoking discussions	**LANGUAGE** Word banks — to describe Billy (before and after) Diaries (Billy's day) Diet sheets — make comparison Interviews for TV and radio — prose and taping Class and group discussions throughout the topic Variety of written work (reporting, imaginative, creative) Write poem entitled 'No more' Sense poem **SPANISH** Descriptive language Healthy foods Hobbies/sports Daily routine Parts of the body

THE EUROPEAN UNION

This is another theme which can be exploited for foreign language work as part of a wider study which may encompass such things as awareness of the countries of the European Union (EU), their key geographical features, their flags, currencies and perhaps some appreciation of their art and music. This, and any visuals, wall displays, etc can prove a valuable stimulus and lead on to work in the foreign language.

Learning aims & objectives

To use the theme of the EU as a vehicle for developing the foreign language.

The following topic areas may be covered:
- *the countries of the EU;*
- *prepositions;*
- *colours;*
- *currencies of the EU;*
- *musical instruments.*

THE COUNTRIES

Knowledge of the countries of the EU, acquired in English, can be reinforced through learning the names in the foreign language.

Their location can also be reinforced. Use a map with the countries numbered, say the name of a country and ask the pupils to identify it by giving the number. Alternatively, a number can be given and the pupils asked to name the country, perhaps from a few possibilities given.

A true/false game can also be played with either the names of the countries themselves or statements about the countries, e.g.:
La France est à côté de l'Espagne. (France is next to Spain.)
L'Espagne est entre le Portugal et La France. (Spain is between Portugal and France.)

You can also cut up a map of the European Union and ask the children to put the pieces together to reform the larger map following instructions in the foreign language, while you point to a position on the board, e.g.:
Ici on peut mettre . . . (Here we can put . . .)
Et là on peut mettre . . . (There we can put . . .)
Alternatively, use or create a large map or perhaps flashcards of countries with

memorable shapes such as Spain, France, Italy, Ireland and lay these on the floor to play a form of the game *Twister*, by giving instructions, such as:
Mettez la main droite sur l'Italie. (Put your right hand on Italy.)

You could also recreate a giant map of Europe on the hall floor, using masking tape, labelling the countries and having the children move 'around Europe'.

THE FLAGS

It is possible to buy mini versions of the flags of the EU countries. Linked together, these can form an attractive display across the room. In one school visited the pupils were involved in a listen and do activity in Spanish — *Ve debajo de la bandera de Italia* (Go under the flag of Italy). The flags can also be used to represent nationalities. There is a more natural link having spoken about the French flag *(le drapeau français)* and used the adjective rather than making the link with a visual representation of the country *(la France)*.

There is a CD-ROM from Vector Europe which can be used to create the flags and many clip art facilities on computers hold examples of numerous flags.

They are also a real and meaningful way to teach, practise or reinforce the pupils' knowledge of colour. A simple listen and draw activity can be devised using a blank template of flags although you have to guard against an excessive amount of time colouring in with little real benefits for language work.

A flag disk is an art and craft/design and technology activity which can be easily modelled and made using some simple instructions. It can be used for any flags but also adapted to include only EU flags. Once made, it can be used for listen and recognition (move the pointer according to instructions given by the teacher or partner) or for a paired speaking exercise in which pupils test the other's knowledge of both flags and the nationalities in the foreign language (see opposite).

CURRENCY

The pupils can be introduced to some of the currencies of Europe and their values in relation to the pound.

This knowledge, combined with a knowledge of numbers in the foreign language, can lead to some purposeful and fun activities involving mental arithmetic, currency conversion and so on, using the foreign language.

Disque de drapeaux

IL VOUS FAUT

du papier	un crayon	une règle
des ciseaux	une attache parisienne	un compas

1. Avec le compas mesurez 9cms.

2. Faites un cercle (rayon 9cms, diamètre 18cms).

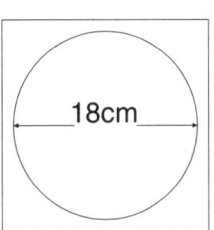
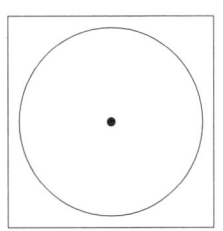

3. Marquez le centre.

4. Divisez le cercle en deux, puis en quatre et enfin en huit.

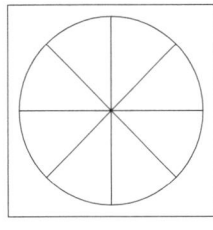
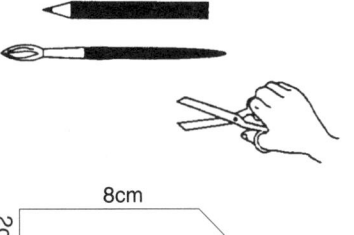

5. Faites une aiguille de 8cms de long et 2cms de large.

6. Dessinez 8 drapeaux dans chaque tranche du cercle.

7. Coloriez les images et l'aiguille.

8. Découpez le cercle et l'aiguille.

9. Attachez l'aiguille au centre avec une attache parisienne.

ET VOILÀ UN DISQUE DE DRAPEAUX!

Music

The pupils may also be made aware of different types of music and instruments in different parts of Europe. Play a short recording and ask the children in the foreign language 'Is that typical of Spain or of Ireland?', thus reinforcing the concept and the language.

There are countless songs which could be taught. *Paule Puhmanns Paddelboot* in particular is an attractive song which includes the greetings of some EU countries.

VOCABULARY

Countries

Le Royaume Uni	The UK	*Le Danemark*	Denmark
Le Portugal	Portugal	*Le Luxembourg*	Luxemburg
La Grèce	Greece	*La France*	France
La Suède	Sweden	*La Finlande*	Finland
La Belgique	Belgium	*L'Irlande*	Ireland
L'Allemagne	Germany	*L'Italie*	Italy
L'Espagne	Spain	*L'Autriche*	Austria
Les Pays-Bas	Netherlands		

Prepositions

A côté de	Beside	*Entre*	Between
A gauche	To the left	*A droite*	To the right

Nationalities

Britannique	British	*Grec/grecque*	Greek
Belge	Belgian	*Portugais(e)*	Portuguese
Français(e)	French	*Hollandais(e)*	Dutch
Irlandais(e)	Irish	*Finlandais(e)*	Finnish
Espagnol(e)	Spanish	*Allemand(e)*	German
Danois(e)	Danish	*Suédois(e)*	Swedish
Italien(ne)	Italian	*Autrichien(ne)*	Austrian
Luxembourgeois(e)	from Luxembourg		

HOUSES

This theme can involve the pupils in work such as looking at different types of houses and their local environment. They may be involved in creating a model and in mathematical work, planning and measuring the model.

Learning aims & objectives

The following aspects could be covered:
- *the rooms of the house;*
- *the furniture;*
- *prepositions;*
- *colours;*
- *adjectives — comparison;*
- *constructing/designing the model house.*

Whereas much of the work will form part of their English language work, it is possible to do some measurements using the foreign language. Making a small item of furniture could be a listen and do activity, following simple instructions in the foreign language and watching the teacher at the same time.

At the decoration stage a lot of real communication could take place as the teacher involves the pupils in deciding on colours. The teacher can offer the pupils the choice of colours illustrating these by coloured paper or by the paintbox.

THE ROOMS AND FURNITURE

The model of the house provides a wonderful resource for the teaching of the various rooms and items of furniture.

Prepositions can be practised in a meaningful way as furniture is placed in different rooms of the house and within the rooms themselves.

Comparison of adjectives could also feature with a comparison of the size of the beds, the chairs, the table, etc.

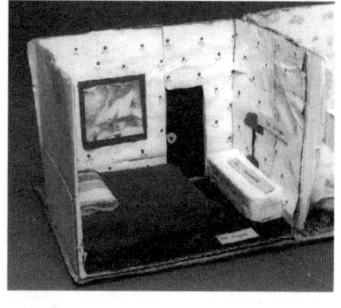

The model can be labelled with the names of the rooms and the furniture itself.

THE INHABITANTS

Whereas the people who live in the house may not actually be created as models, the house itself gives a meaningful context for talking about its imaginary inhabitants. This is a similar process to that described in Chapter 2 and of course the house could easily form part of the village theme.

The rooms, furniture and inhabitants could of course be discussed by using a ready made model house, but using something which has involved the pupils own work can add to the motivation.

VOCABULARY

Rooms

le salon	lounge	*la salle à manger*	dining room
le vestibule	hall	*la salle de séjour*	living room
la chambre	bedroom	*la salle de bain(s)*	bathroom
la cuisine	kitchen		

Furniture

le fauteuil	armchair	*le sofa/canapé*	sofa
le lit	bed	*l'armoire*	wardrobe
la table	table	*la baignoire*	bath
la chaise	chair	*la télé*	TV
la lampe	lamp	*la cuisinière*	cooker
la machine à laver	washing machine		

Colours

jaune	yellow	*rouge*	red	*rose*	pink
gris(e)	grey	*bleu(e)*	blue	*vert(e)*	green
noir(e)	black	*blanc(he)*	white		

Adjectives — comparison

grand(e)	big	*petit(e)*	small
moyen(ne)	medium	*plus*	more
moins	less		

OTHER THEMES

Teachers have been very inventive in using existing projects to act as a stimulus for language work. In addition to the above I particularly remember the childrens' wall display of their visit to the Sea Life centre used as a stimulus for related language work on animals; the history display for work on self and descriptive language — yes, describing Bonnie Prince Charlie and Flora Macdonald in German!

There is also the use of the study of clothes and fashion inspired by a visit to a local clothes factory. Here the pupils were learning about textiles through the medium of English. However, the paper clothes line hung out across the classroom was a magnificent way of teaching/talking about clothes. This also led onto related language work for clothes such as a fashion show with the clothes being described in the foreign language. If one wished to integrate a story into this theme, then the traditional tale of *The Emperor's new clothes* would seem to fit.

THE BOOK AS THE THEME

Pupils may be involved in the study of a book in English. The book may have provided the stimulus for related work in art and craft/design and technology and a wall display may have been created. In a similar way, it can also offer opportunities for foreign language work.

To take the example of Colin Dann's *The Animals of Farthing Wood* (published by Mammoth), this could provide a context for animals and for descriptive language relating to the countryside and for expressions such as 'he is hungry', 'he is tired', 'he is afraid'.

Unlike in storytelling, it is not suggested that this story itself is told in the foreign language, but rather that it can provide a good framework for related work. The children are more likely to remember the animals being tired or hungry than if these expressions are taught in isolation.

The Scottish Office Education and Industry Department's training programme provides another good example: *Carrie's war* by Nina Bawden (Puffin books). The characters can be used for descriptive language. The story includes a train journey, so clothes (packing the case) and travel can be covered. Nick has a birthday party, so that leads to food and drink.

This chapter has considered using an existing theme as a context for the foreign language. It is important to remember, however, that not all themes lend themselves to this approach and the teacher has to evaluate the linguistic potential in each case. Where it does exist, there is no doubt that it is a beneficial approach and a powerful motivator.

4 Festivals

One of the easiest links is to common festivals such as Christmas, Easter and Halloween. The teacher may explain some of the key points about the festival in the country or countries whose language is being studied. This may be done in English with perhaps the introduction of some key phrases in the foreign language. It is also possible to link the themes using related listen and do activities, songs, stories, etc.

Learning aims & objectives

To use the theme of festivals as a vehicle for developing the foreign language and cultural awareness.

The following topic areas may be covered:

- *colours;*
- *numbers;*
- *weather;*
- *clothes;*
- *alphabet;*
- *flowers/plants.*

CHRISTMAS

MAKING THINGS

There are some ideas in *Games and fun activities (YPF2)* by Cynthia Martin. These include a robin and a Christmas card.

It is also possible to make mobiles incorporating e.g. a snowman, Father Christmas, a Christmas tree. By using a grid figure with numbers and/or letters these could be coloured according to the teachers' instructions and provide a colourful classroom display (see opposite).

For example,
Coloriez 1 en rouge (Colour 1 red)

Der Weihnachtsbaum

Another excellent idea in the Scottish training programme for German involves the pupils in a Christmas board game which could also be made by the pupils (see pp26–27).

In addition to the board itself they create cards. In the German version these are divided into snowmen, stars and trees with each category of card being either a simple sum, a simple question or a puzzle, e.g. say a word beginning with (. . .) (see p27).

If pupils land on a snowman square, they take a card from the pile. If they answer successfully, they go forward, e.g. two spaces. If the answer is wrong, then it is a backward move on the board.

Weihnachtsbrettspiel

Schneemannkärtchen

Suche ein Wort, das mit F beginnt.

Suche ein Wort, das mit J beginnt.

Suche ein Wort, das mit L beginnt.

Suche ein Wort, das mit T beginnt.

Suche ein Wort, das mit R beginnt.

Suche ein Wort, das mit M beginnt.

It is also a good idea to make an advent calendar. The children make the (numbered) doors and windows and draw any object for which they have the foreign language word/expression, each thus making their own personalised calendar. The language is revealed when all the doors/windows have been opened and they look at each other's calendars. They present their calendars with the language and then 'test' their partner's memory as to what is behind each door/window.

SONGS AND CAROLS

There are so many possibilities and the children enjoy singing in the foreign language which is more easily remembered this way. Some of the best songs include *Mon beau sapin, Douce nuit, Sainte nuit* in French; *Stille Nacht* and *Wir bauen einen Schneeman* in German; *Noche de Paz* and *Campanas de Belén* in Spanish and *Santo Natale* and *Tu scendi dalle stelle* in Italian.

Santo Natal! Notte d'amor!
Tutto tace il cielo è d'or,
Già distende la luna il suo vel,
'Gloria' cantano gli Angeli in ciel,
nella misera grotta
nasce il Bambino Gesù!

Santo Natal! Notte d'amor!
Una bianca stella appar
al richiamo Re Magi e pastor
sono accorsi a pregare il Signor,
con la Vergine madre
dorme il Fanciullo Divin.

STORYTELLING

There is an obvious and wonderful story for Christmastime: The snowman by Raymond Briggs. It is a rich resource for language development covering a wide variety of language areas such as food, weather, clothes. If it is possible to use the televised version, a simple commentary could be added in the foreign language as the pictures convey so much meaning.

Another story by Raymond Briggs, Father Christmas, may also be useful.

OTHER FESTIVALS

EASTER

As with Christmas, the teacher can explain any key points. Springtime may be a good time for considering the weather, the flowers and plants. Such a study could offer potential for related work in the foreign language.

Using the same principles of simple, easy to follow instructions, combined with good illustrations or modelling, it is another opportunity for a listen and do activity.

Joyeuses Pâques!

The Spanish training programme contains a simple attractive idea for an Easter bunny carrying Easter eggs (see p30).

El rollo conejo

NECESITÁIS
una hoja con el modelo
un rollo (tubo)
tijeras
rotuladores
papel pegante amarillo
pegamento
un poco de algodón
un huevo de pascua

1. Forrad el rollo con papel pegante amarillo.
2. Coloread el conejo y los pies de amarillo.
3. Coloread la zanahoria de naranja.
4. Recortad el conejo, los pies y la zanahoria.
5. Pegad el conejo en el rollo y la zanahoria en las manos.
6. Pegad un poco de algodón detrás. Es la cola.
7. Poned el huevo de pascua dentro del rollo.

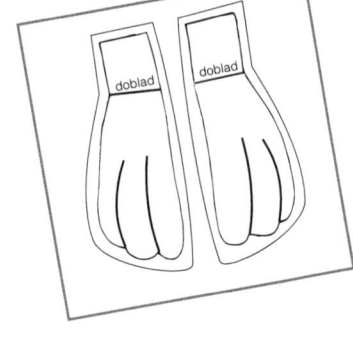

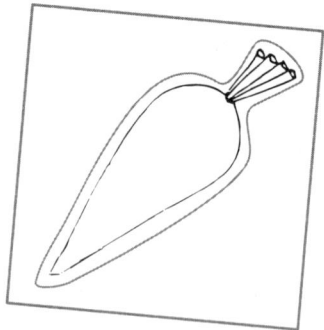

delante

detrás

HALLOWEEN/SHROVETIDE

These are good occasions for pupils to dress up and do related work on clothes, such as describing the clothes they are wearing, e.g. colour, size, etc.

Qu'est-ce qu'il/elle porte? (What is he/she wearing?)
De quelle couleur est la chemise? (What colour is the shirt?)

Work on clothes may also lead to dressing up cardboard figures according to the instructions of a partner, or the outfits could be used in a fun fashion parade with a commentary being prepared in French.

Pupils could play a memory game after they have changed back to normal clothing, answering questions such as 'Who was wearing jeans, a checked shirt and a cowboy hat? Who was dressed as a tennis player with white shorts and a blue T-shirt?'

Jobs could be combined with the language of clothes. The children could be encouraged to dress up in a halloween outfit representing different jobs, e.g. baker, nurse, etc. These costumes could then be used for work relating to those jobs, places of work and the clothes worn, e.g.:

Il est boulanger. Où est-ce qu'il travaille? Qu'est-ce qu'il porte? (He is a baker. Where does he work? What is he wearing?)

The children could learn a *comptine* or a song for their mini performance.

Again, listen and do activities may be devised such as making a mask (see p32).

Of course there may also be local festivals to which language work can be linked.

Una maschera da un sacchetto di carta

MATERIALE

sacchetti di carta bianca
carta velina colorata
forbici
colla
scotch
pennarelli

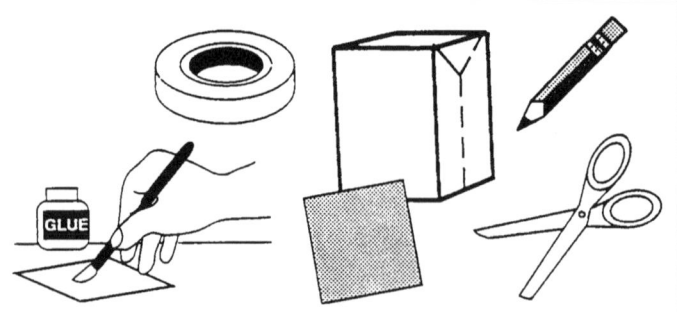

ISTRUZIONI

Prendete un sacchetto di carta bianca.

Disegnate gli occhi in posizione giusta.

Ritagliate gli occhi.

Disegnate una faccia su un lato del sacchetto.

Colorate con i pennarelli.

Se volete aggiungete . . . una corona

capelli fatti di lana tagliata o carta tagliata a strisce.

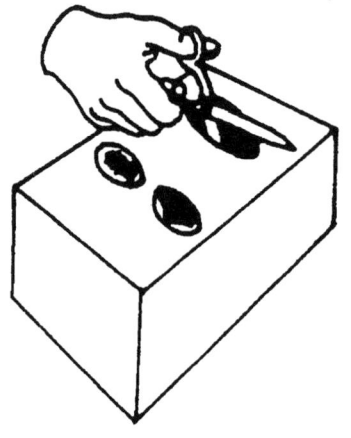

VOCABULARY

Colouring
Coloriez 1 en rouge — Colour 1 red — FOR A LIST OF COMMON COLOURS SEE CHAPTER 3

The seasons
En été	in summer	*En automne*	in autumn
En hiver	in winter	*Au printemps*	in spring

The weather
Il fait chaud	it is hot	*Il fait du soleil*	it is sunny
Il fait froid	it is cold	*Il fait du brouillard*	it is foggy
Il fait beau	it is fine	*Il fait mauvais*	it is bad
Il neige	it snows	*Il pleut*	it rains

Clothes
Le pantalon	trousers	*Le jean*	jeans
Le T-shirt	T-shirt	*Le pull-over*	pullover
Le chemisier	blouse	*Le chapeau*	hat
La chemise	shirt	*La jupe*	skirt
La robe	dress	*L'écharpe*	scarf
Les chaussures	shoes	*Les chaussettes*	socks

5. Linking the foreign language to curriculum subjects

This chapter offers suggestions for combining some foreign language work with activities from various curriculum subjects. The intention here is to illustrate ways in which foreign language work might occasionally be integrated into the 'normal' mother-tongue work of the classroom by the class teacher who has some knowledge of the foreign language, but not necessarily the proficiency and fluency to conduct a lesson entirely in the target language. Chapter 6 will take this integration a step further and provide worked-up suggestions for delivering curriculum activities entirely through the foreign language. Although there is some commonality between activities presented in this chapter and those in Chapter 6, those which follow in this chapter involve less, and less complex, foreign language, though some teachers may wish to move between Chapters 5 and 6 to select activities for their own schemes of work.

 MATHEMATICS

During numeracy practice sessions, or as a ten-minute activity at the start or end of the day, a variety of mental maths activities can be done in the foreign language by combining numbers with a minimum of additional vocabulary:

VOCABULARY			
plus	plus	moins	minus
x fois y	x multiplied by y	x divisé par y	x divided by y
égalent	equals		

SURVEYS

Pupils can do basic survey work through the foreign language:

- exchanging family (and other) details in the foreign language: *Tu as combien de frères?* (How many brothers have you got?);
- the months in which birthdays fall (*C'est quel mois, ton anniversaire?*);
- favourite foods and drinks (*Qu'est-ce que tu préfères manger/boire?*);
- favourite hobbies (*Quels sont tes passe-temps favoris?*);
- pets (*Tu as un animal à la maison?*);

and in order to provide a reason to listen and record, the data gathered can be presented in charts and graphs, either by sticking coloured squares to form column graphs, or by using a computer 'chart' program.

SHAPES

Earlier work on naming shapes can be re-visited in the foreign language:

- pupils have various shapes available in their groups and hold up/bring out shapes on request, e.g. a triangle, a circle and a rectangle (*Montrez-moi/apportez-moi un triangle, un cercle, un rectangle . . .*);

- combine the language of shapes with that of numbers and colours: pupils are given a selection of coloured paper from which to cut shapes to order — three yellow rectangles, one green and one blue rectangle (*Découpez trois rectangles jaunes, un rectangle vert et un rectangle bleu*).

VOCABULARY

Surveys

Tu as combien de frères?	How many brothers do you have?
C'est quel mois ton anniversaire?	In which month do you have your birthday?
Qu'est-ce que tu aimes manger?	What do you like to eat?
Qu'est-ce que tu aimes boire?	What do you like to drink?
Quel est ton passe-temps favori?	What is your favourite hobby?
Tu as un animal à la maison?	Do you have a pet?

Shapes

un triangle	a triangle	*un carré*	a square
un rectangle	a rectangle	*un ovale*	an oval
un cercle	a circle		

Shapes and colours

Apportez-moi	Bring me	*4 cercles bleus*	4 blue circles
Montrez-moi	Show me	*5 ovales jaunes*	5 yellow ovals
2 triangles verts	2 green triangles	*6 rectangles rouges*	6 red rectangles
3 carrés roses	3 pink squares		

ENGLISH (KNOWLEDGE ABOUT LANGUAGE)

The benefits of learning a foreign language to the development of knowledge about the first language are well documented, and the class teacher who is responsible for language development is well-placed to make the link. Comparing the features of first and second language is one good way to increase language awareness, e.g.:

- when the concepts of parts of speech and their names have been established in English (noun, verb, adjective . . .), these can be revisited in the foreign language: pupils are asked to identify the role of words in simple foreign language sentences (e.g. by pointing to key words on a display on the board/wall; by colour-coding; by word tabs which can be arranged in part-of-speech sets);

- rules and patterns (and the similarities and differences which occur between languages in this respect) can be discerned through word lists, e.g. word endings to denote gender in Italian: *fratello* (brother), *fratella* (sister); suffixes in Spanish to denote size: *un vaso* (glass), *un vasito* (little glass); the article in French: *le père* (father), *la mère* (mother), etc;

- if there are bilingual children in the class, they can be asked to provide examples of rules and patterns in a language they know (how languages indicate possession, e.g. the 's in English, is a fruitful area).

DICTIONARY SKILLS

Show pupils how the first part of the dictionary is in one language and the second half in the other. Take them through an English dictionary first by asking them to turn over, say, ten pages at a time and to tell you which letter they have arrived at. Eventually they will arrive at the end of the dictionary. Now repeat the process with a foreign language dictionary. As they near the end of the alphabet for the first section, or cross over into the second section, highlight the difference.

Using the English–French section, ask a pupil to suggest a fruit. Guide the whole class to that entry in the correct section. Then play a game asking them in groups to find the names of five fruits in French. Set a time limit. See what the pupils have found by writing up some of the words for fruits on the board. Some different words for the same fruit may emerge.

Use these as a vehicle for demonstrating the cross-referencing aspect by guiding them to looking up the different words in the French–English section before coming to an agreement on which version is correct.

For more ideas on developing dictionary skills see Berwick G and P Horsfall, *Making effective use of the dictionary (PF28)* (CILT, 1996).

GEOGRAPHY

Chapter 3 gave examples of using the European Union as a theme. Other links with Geography can be made, e.g.:

- place names and map co-ordinates;

- symbols representing features to place on maps (e.g. mountains, forests, airports — see Chapter 6 for further exploitation);

- *Twister*: a large map is placed on the floor. There are two sets of cards: words for parts of the body — *la main* (hand), *le pied* (foot), *le genou* (knee), *la tête* (head); words for towns/countries/continents. Pupils choose one card from each set and follow the instruction (which the teacher reinforces orally): *Mettez la main gauche sur les Etats-Unis . . .*;

- studies of countries: features dealt with can be repeated in the foreign language, perhaps involving home-produced maps for display; information can be tested using true/false games in the foreign language: *la capitale de la France, c'est Marseille?*; distances between major towns.

DESIGN AND TECHNOLOGY

- Making a weather disk (another activity featured in the Scottish training programme): the disk when made can be used to practise phrases to describe the weather;

Wetterkreis

ES WIRD GEBRAUCHT
ein Blatt Papier   ein Lineal   eine Schere
eine Heftklammer   ein Bleistift   ein Zirkel
Farbstifte

1 Mit dem Zirkel miß 9cm.

2 Zeichne einen Kreis (Radius 9cm, Durchmesser 18cm).

3 Zeichne den Mittelpunkt.

4 Teile den Kreis in zwei Hälften. Teile ihn noch einmal-es entstehen vier Viertel und noch einmal-es entstenen acht Achtel.

5 Mache einen Zeiger 8cm lang und 2cm breit.

6 Zeichne 8 Bilder.

| Es ist schön | Es ist kalt | Es ist windig | Es ist neblig |
| Es schneit | Es regnet | Es blitzt | Es ist wolkig |

7 Male die Bilder und den Zeiger schön an.

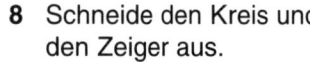

8 Schneide den Kreis und den Zeiger aus.

9 Mache den Zeiger mit derm Musterklammer in der Mitte des Kreises fest.

UND JETZT HAST DU EINEN WETTERKREIS! WIE IST DAS WETTER?

- Making a cardboard caterpillar: the story of *The very hungry caterpillar* is popular in schools. This craft activity (included in the Scottish Italian and Spanish training programmes) relates to it.

Il bruco affamato

MATERIALE

2 cartoni per uova   forbici
pennarelli   cura-pipe
fermacarte   blu-tack

(Work in groups of 3 or 4)

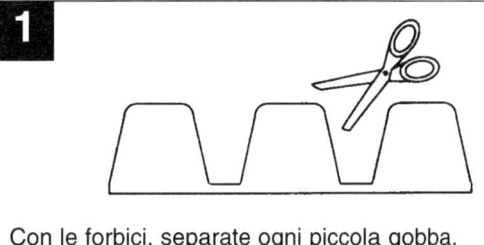

Con le forbici, separate ogni piccola gobba.

Prendete 2 gobbe ciascuno e decoratele con i pennarelli.

Inserite un fermacarte in ogni gobba per riunirle.

Ora, riunite tutte le gobbe fatte dal gruppo.

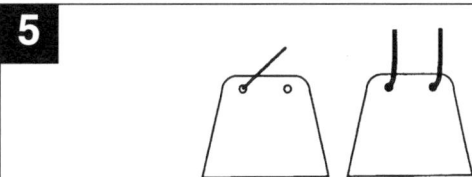

Prendete un'altra gobba e fate due piccoli buchi. Inserite una cura-pipa in ogni buco.

Con il blu-tack fate due palloncini e attaccateli alle cura-pipe.

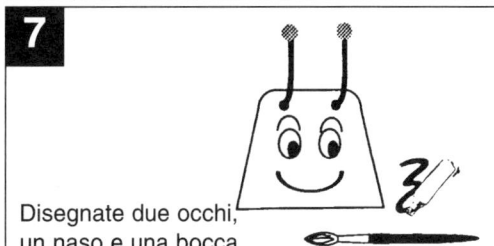

Disegnate due occhi, un naso e una bocca.

Riunite le parti del corpo alla testa. Ora fate una bella passeggiata con **Il Bruco Affamato**.

Physical education

- Familiar warm-up and aerobics activities can be done with instructions given in the foreign language;

- the four corner game: one of four cards is placed in each corner of the gym (e.g. clock faces representing different times). Pupils select and run to a corner. The teacher calls out the phrase indicating one of the corners, e.g. *il est six heures et demie* (it's six thirty). Pupils who have chosen the wrong corner are 'out'. Those remaining are given an instruction such as *Sautez cinq fois* (jump five times), before being told again *Choisissez un coin* (choose a corner) and the process is repeated until one pupil remains;

- fruit bowl: chairs (numbering one fewer than participants) are placed in a circle and pupils sit on them. One pupil stands in the centre and says: *levez-vous si vous avez les yeux bleus*. Pupils with blue eyes are required to change seats while the pupil in the middle tries to occupy an empty chair. The pupil left without a chair assumes the centre role (can be a lively, competitive game!);

- indoor action games can be done in the gym with more freedom of movement;

- 'Head and shoulders, knees and toes': to the tune of *There is a tavern in the town*, pupils touch corresponding parts of the body while singing. Other suitable action songs are *Hokey Cokey* and *Boogie Woogie*.

> *Cabeza, hombros,*
> *piernas, pies*
> *piernas, pies*
> *Cabeza, hombros,*
> *piernas, pies*
> *piernas, pies*
> *Oreja, ojos,*
> *boca y nariz*
> *Cabeza, hombros,*
> *piernas, pies*
> *piernas, pies.*

Music

Songs have the advantage of enabling pupils to encounter chunks of language in contexts (which can often be conveyed by pictures) rather than single words. Examples in frequent use include:

(French):   *Frère Jacques; Coccinelle; Vent frais; Chevaliers de la table ronde; Sur le pont d'Avignon*;
(German):   *Laurentia; Lied, Wenn du fröhlich bist; Dornröschen; Heut kommt der Hans nach Haus*;
(Italian):   *O Bella Ciao; La zia di Forli;*
(Spanish):   *La Bamba, Cielito Lindo, Guantanamera.*

There are many commercial sources for songs. Among those commonly used are: *Le français en chantant, Eine kleine Deutschmusik* and songs from the Berlitz *Just for kids* series. Some schools have created their own songs or adapted existing ones. The performance of songs, e.g. in assembly, in school performances for parents, etc gives status to foreign language learning.

Drama

Stories can be re-scripted as playlet dialogues with characters and a narrator, e.g. *Goldilocks*. Drama diminishes pupils inhibitions about using the foreign language; they are often more comfortable in the guise of a character than as themselves.

Role play scenes can involve props made in school, e.g. at the café, at the market, on the beach.

All these suggested activities find a link with other areas of the curriculum, though the prime intention is to give the mother-tongue teaching some additional foreign language content. Confident practitioners can take this notion of involving the foreign language in curriculum work a stage further, to something nearer 'teaching other subjects through the medium of the foreign language'. This more advanced work is the subject of the next chapter.

6. Extending the link — and the learner

This final chapter of the book is a collection of materials produced for an in-service training course for Oxfordshire primary teachers.[1] The intention of the course was to provide ideas, materials and a sample methodology to help primary teachers who were not trained modern language specialists to use French as the medium for teaching aspects of the National Curriculum subjects and RE.

From an initial glance at the material in this chapter, some readers may feel that the language content is ambitious — indeed, that it is more demanding than the early years of secondary school. It is true that the vocabulary is rich and sometimes idiomatic, and some structures are complex. It needs to be stressed, however, that by no means all of this language is expected to be functionally mastered by pupils. It is sufficient and worthwhile, in our judgment, for pupils to be exposed to language which will give them a head start in sound recognition and production, an ease and confidence in dealing with extensive target language use, and an awareness that acute listening is a prerequisite for good language learning. We would expect these benefits to be real, even for pupils who had experienced primary French for two years before going on to study Spanish or German in Key Stage 3 rather than French.

It was a requirement for participation on the course that teachers should have:

- an ability to pronounce French in a way which approximated to native-speaker use and which was not unduly 'contaminated' by the sounds of English;
- some building on 'O' level (or equivalent) standards either through experience or further study.

We felt that with this level of expertise and the support of these sample materials, teachers would have the knowledge and confidence both to use these materials and to develop similar activities themselves.

---

1. A group of twenty teachers in Oxfordshire LEA primary schools took part in the course which the LEA commissioned in 1996. The course was devised and led by Ann Miller (then of Westminster College Oxford, now of the University of Leicester) whose contribution to this book is gratefully acknowledged. We would also like to thank the following colleagues from Westminster College Oxford: *David Coates, Shirley Dobson, Béatrice Davies, Jenny Gray, John Halocha, Susan Hector, Margaret Jones, David Mende, Christina Skarbek, Paul Taylor and Patricia Thompson.*

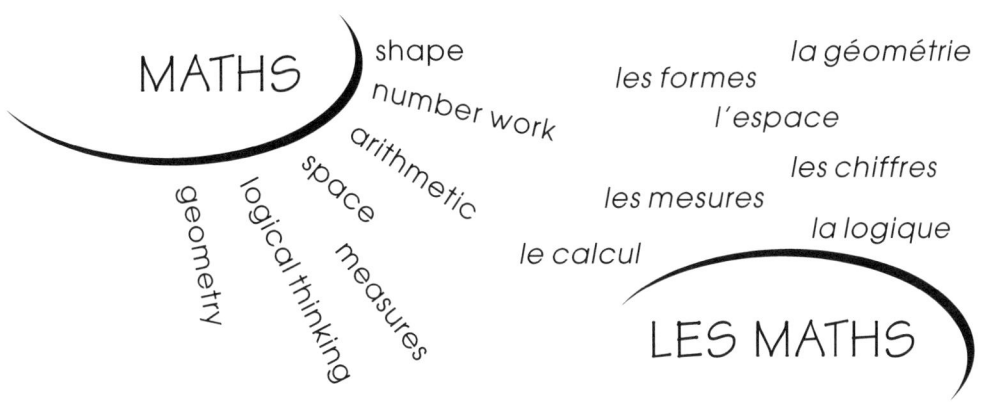

MATHEMATICS

This chapter exemplifies work drawn from the NC for England and Wales *Key Stage 2 Mathematics (NC pages 26–35):*

and the coverage offered by the activities is as follows:
Number (3a,c,d)
Shape, Space and Measures (2b, 3a, 3b, 4a,). These are activities which children will have experienced in English and are repeating here in French.

Learning aims & objectives

Maths

Basic practice and consolidation is provided in the mental computation of numbers and the exploration of number sequences, using mathematics in practical tasks, checking results, understanding of the properties of shapes, considering patterns, describing shapes and movements, using appropriate measures accurately, estimating size and weight.

French

Pupils hear and understand (and sometimes use):
- *imperatives (to follow instructions);*
- *language to describe shapes, measures;*
- *some useful phrases for common classroom language: in turn, get into groups, anyone who wants to . . . , you must start again, etc;*
- *numbers: 1–100.*

ACTIVITIES

Once the words for numbers from 1–20 are known, there are numerous games which can be used for practice, e.g.:

One-at-a-time (number)

Pupils (in groups of four or five) are invited to count individually from one to twenty, each saying one number, but without two or more pupils speaking together. If two pupils say the same number together, the count must start again. You monitor.
Mettez-vous en groupes de quatre (cinq). Essayez de compter jusqu'à vingt; c'est à qui le veut de commencer en disant 'un', à qui le veut de continuer en disant 'deux' et ainsi de suite. Mais si deux personnes parlent en même temps, il faut recommencer.

Counting for softies (number)

Counting around the class while throwing a soft toy.
X commence et dit 'un'. Elle (il) jette la peluche à quelqu'un qui doit dire 'deux' et ainsi de suite.

Count and gesture (number)

Pupils count aloud, but as they do so, they associate each number with a gesture. Successive pupils must remember the gestures as well as continue the numbering.
On va compter de un jusqu'à vingt, mais pour chaque numéro on va faire un geste . . .

Bip (number)

Counting aloud, but replacing every fifth (or another interval) number by 'bip' or the French version of a door-bell chime 'bim bam'.
On va compter à tour de rôle. Allez: un (Emma), deux (Zoe), trois (Darren), quatre (Joe). Mais Richard, tu ne dis pas cinq, tu dis 'bip', d'accord? Et on continue . . . six (James) . . .

Human numbers (number)

Ten pupils, each carrying a number from zero to nine, stand in front of the rest of the class. As you call out (and later a pupil calls out) a two-digit number, the pupils with the appropriate numbers have to stand forward and arrange themselves properly.

Je vais dire un numéro, par exemple, vingt-neuf. Quels numéros faut-il pour faire le vingt-neuf? Oui, c'est ça, le deux et le neuf. Alors les élèves qui ont la carte deux et la carte neuf, prenez un pas en avant. Voilà! Mettez-vous comme ça.

The price is right (number)

Le Juste prix — a game on the lines of *The price is right.* Before this activity, pupils need to be aware of the relationship between French francs and the £. Maths can feature easily in teaching this, using 10 francs = £1 as the rate of exchange. If you have some facsimile money, so much the better. You call out a number of francs, pupils calculate in pounds: Teacher: *60 francs?* Pupil(s): *6 livres.* (Deal with the pronunciation changes which occur when numbers are used alone, and when followed by a noun: *six, dix*). Reverse the process; then pupils can challenge each other.

Play this in two stages, with the class divided into two teams:
(1) various objects are on display at the front of the class — anything will do . . . a pencil-case, handkerchief, pen, toy. Each object has a concealed price tag, and also two (or three) slips of paper next to it (e.g. 3 and 5) turned upwards. One pupil from each team has to guess the price of each object: *53 francs ou 35 francs?*
(2) play without the 'guide' numbers. Each object has a concealed price tag; one member from each team estimates the price. The closer wins the point.
Equipe A: Emily, devine le prix du stylo . . . combien ça coûte?

Rub it out (number)

Divide the board into two with a vertical line. Write numbers in each half: each number must appear on both sides, but in a different place. One pupil from each team stands in front of the board with a piece of chalk or a boardwriter and tries to be first to cross out each number called by the teacher.

Some possible demonstration language:
Je divise le tableau en deux, comme ça, avec un trait. Je vais mettre des numéros des deux côtés — les mêmes numéros, vouz voyez . . . 36 ici, et 36 ici. Voilà. Bon; il y a deux équipes . . . un élève de chaque équipe se tient devant le tableau comme ça, un feutre (une craie) à la main. Je vais appeler un numéro. Il faut trouver le numéro et le barrer (mime).

Tour de France (number)

Before this activity you will need to introduce the notion that metropolitan France is divided into 95 *départements* (= counties), and you will need a map of them (with the numbers appearing on the map and the numbered names appearing as a separate key), either big enough to display on the board or on an OHT. Some of the names of the *départements* may be unwieldy for pupils. If so, you will need to use them for recognition only, while children produce the associated numbers. Teach them 'zéro-un', for 01, etc. You call out a *département* name, pupils have to supply its number. Then move to an activity in which two pupils at the board compete to be first to point out on the map the *département* whose name you call out:

On a une carte de la France avec les départements. Voici les départements avec les numéros . . . et voici les noms des départements avec les numéros. Un élève de chaque équipe se tient de chaque côté de la carte. Je vais dire le nom d'un département. Pour gagner un point il faut être le premier à toucher le département sur la carte.

Rank and file (number — relationships between numbers)

You need to teach *grand, petit* and *plus grand, plus petit* first. This activity needs space to move — perhaps the hall rather than a classroom. Pupils line up in rank and file, e.g. five (six) by five (six). You give each pupil a red and a yellow card. Pupils in the first column write 1 on their card, those in column 2 write 2 on their card, and so on. Pupils in row 1 write 1 on their yellow card, row 2 write 2 on their yellow card and so on. Give instructions such as: 'yellow number 3s, stay standing, others all sit down; red and yellow numbers bigger than 4, sit down . . . ; add your red number to your yellow number — if the total is greater than 9 . . .' and so on.

On va faire une grille. Mettez-vous en cinq (six) rangs de cinq (six) personnes. Je vais donner une carte rouge ou une carte jaune à chaque personne. Voilà la première colonne, écrivez 1 sur la carte rouge. La deuxième colonne, écrivez 2 sur la carte rouge . . . (etc). Le premier rang, écrivez 1 sur la carte jaune. Le deuxième rang, écrivez 2 sur la carte jaune . . . (etc).

la première colonne: le premier rang:

```
(x  x  x  x  x)         (x  x  x  x  x)
 x  x  x  x  x           x  x  x  x  x
 x  x  x  x  x           x  x  x  x  x
 x  x  x  x  x           x  x  x  x  x
 x  x  x  x  x           x  x  x  x  x
```

Maintenant, écoutez attentivement, et suivez les instructions. Si le numéro jaune est 3, restez debout. Les autres, asseyez-vous (make as if to check). OK, levez-vous.

Si le numéro rouge est 5, restez debout. Les autres, asseyez-vous (make as if to check). OK, levez-vous.

Restez debout si le numéro jaune est 2 ou plus grand que 2. Les autres, asseyez-vous.
Restez debout si le numéro rouge est 4, ou plus petit que 4.
Restez debout si les numéros rouge et jaune sont plus grands que 4.
Restez debout si les numéros rouge et jaune sont plus petits que 3.

Additionnez le numéro rouge et le numéro jaune (le numéro rouge plus le numéro jaune). Si le total est plus grand que 9 (plus petit que 4, etc), restez debout.

Asseyez-vous si votre numéro rouge est plus grand que votre numéro jaune. Multipliez votre numéro rouge par votre numéro jaune. Si le total est plus grand que 10, asseyez-vous . . . (etc)

On the map (shape, space and measures)

Prepare a map of France with coordinates (perhaps on an OHP overlay): and a number of cities marked and named.

Voici une carte de France avec des villes marquées et . . . regardez . . . il y a aussi des coordonnées dessus. Alors dites-moi . . . quelle ville se trouve dans la case C3? Dans la case E5?

(Pupils could take over the teacher's role, once they have grasped the idea and the words).

	a	b	c	d	e
1					
2					
3					
4					
5					

Shape up (shape, space and measure)

Before this activity it will be necessary to teach pupils the words for geometric shapes. This can be done by 'point/identify/say/repeat', by cutting out and labelling, by miming the shape and getting pupils to draw, trace, use stencils, etc. Packets of adhesive shapes are useful.

The minimum needed are: *un cercle, un carré, un triangle, un rectangle (un losange — diamond)*. Also possible are: *un ovale, un trapèze, un parallélépipède*.

They also need to know *à droite, à gauche, au milieu* which you can demonstrate by moving objects (and children!) around.

 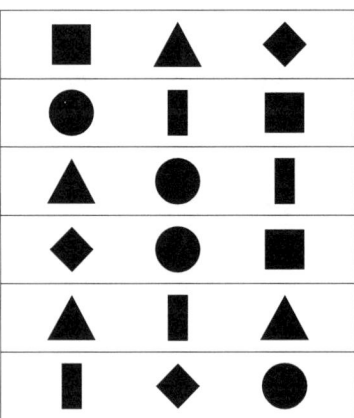

Pupils follow your instructions by drawing in the required shapes, then at the end they compare their results with your original grid.

Dans la première case, dessinez un carré à gauche, un triangle au milieu et un losange à droite. Dans la deuxième case . . . etc.

Animal shapes (shape, space and measures)

Using the same vocabulary, pupils could design animals and objects on graph paper, using only the geometric shapes given. They then say what they have drawn and how it is composed. *C'est un oiseau. Il y a deux losanges, deux cercles, deux rectangles . . .*

An alternative version of the same activity:
Give each small group of pupils (or have them cut out) ten squares, ten circles, ten

rectangles and ten triangles and challenge them to make all the objects in the list: *(Dans chaque groupe, vous allez découper dix carrés, dix cercles, dix rectangles, et dix triangles). Maintenant, avec les formes que vous avez, faites: une voiture, un bateau, deux maisons avec le soleil au milieu, une usine, un train.* (A solution is possible).

Mosaics (shape, space and measures) / *Les mosaïques*

Teachers involved with maths will be familiar with activities involving mirror-image patterns of mosaics — tesselations — e.g. Moorish tile designs. Coloured versions can be used, but in order to introduce some language, pupils write in the words for the mirror-image colours in the appropriate spaces.

Ecrivez le nom de la couleur de chaque triangle dans la partie droite.

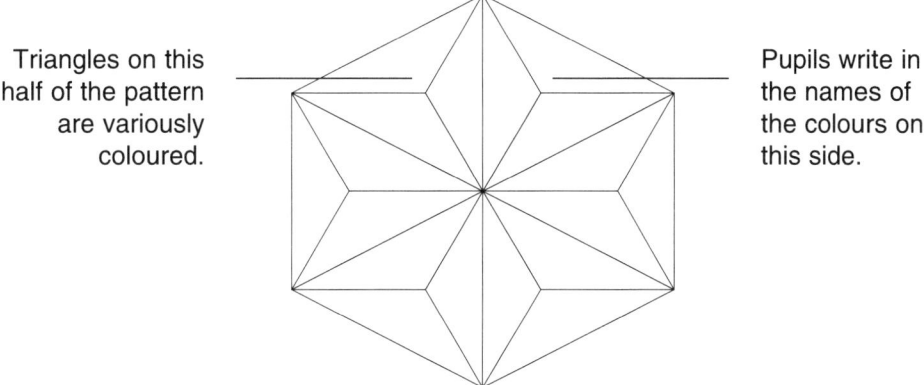

Triangles on this half of the pattern are variously coloured.

Pupils write in the names of the colours on this side.

Guess my weight (shape, space and measures) / *Les estimations*

Once pupils have been introduced to weight in kilogrammes and grammes and linear measure in metres and centimetres, they can proceed to various estimate-then-measure activities.

Have children bring in something to weigh, e.g soft toys. *On va estimer le poids de cet ours. Il pèse combien de grammes?* (If there is a collection of bears, pupils can estimate and then rank them in weight order.) *On va peser l'ours pour voir qui a raison ou qui est le plus proche.*

You can proceed similarly for length. *On va maintenant estimer la taille des ours. Cet ours, il mesure combien de centimètres?*

And also time: *On va estimer vingt secondes. Ne regardez pas vos montres, ne regardez pas l'horloge. Je vais dire à vos marques, prêts, partez! Après vingt secondes, levez le doigt.*

Rocket (shape, space and measures) / *La fusée*

Following instructions, pupils make and fly a paper dart, then measure the distance it travels. (A pupil could give the instructions, second time through.)

Prenez une feuille de papier rectangulaire. Pliez-la en deux. Dépliez-la.
Pliez les bords x et y vers le centre.
Retournez la fusée. Pliez les bords a et b vers le centre.
Pliez la fusée en deux le long du premier pliage. Ecartez les ailes pour lui donner la forme d'une fusée.
Lancez la fusée en l'air. Marquez l'endroit où elle atterrit. Mesurez la distance qu'elle a parcourue.

VOCABULARY

Le langage de la salle de classe	Classroom language
s'asseoir (asseyez-vous)	sit down
à tour de rôle	take turns
c'est à qui le veut de . . .	who want to . . .
la colonne	the column
comme ça	like this/that
continuez	continue
la craie	the chalk
d'accord	OK
écrire	write
écrivez	write!
léquipe (f)	team
essayez de . . .	try to . . .
et ainsi de suite	and so on . . .
le feutre	felt
faire un geste	make a gesture
la grille	the grill
gagner un point	win a point
il faut (faut-il?)	you have to (have you?)

se lever (levez-vous)	stand up
levez le doigt	lift a finger
mettez-vous en groups de . . .	get into groups of . . .
par exemple	for example
le rang	row
recommencer	start again
rester debout	stay standing
suivre (suivez) les instructions	follow the instructions
se tenir (devant le tableau)	stand in front of the board
toucher	touch
voilà	there you are

Les maths — **Maths**

aditioner	to add
aditioner	add!
ajouter	to add up
le carré	the square
combien (çoûte?)	how much does that cost
compter	to count
comptez	count!
les coordonnées	the coordinates
les chiffres (de 1 à 100)	the numbers (from 1 to 100)
deviner	to quess
devine(z)	guess!
la distance (parcourue)	distance (route)
diviser	divide
la forme	the shape
le gramme	the gram
le kilogramme	the kilogram
le long de	the length of
le losange	the losenge (diamond shaped)
multiplier	multiply
paralléle	parallel
plus (grand, petit)	more (bigger than, smaller than)
peser	wiegh
pliage	folding
plier	to fold
pliez	fold!
le poids	the wieght
le rectangle	the recatangle
rectangulaire	rectangular
le triangle	the triangle

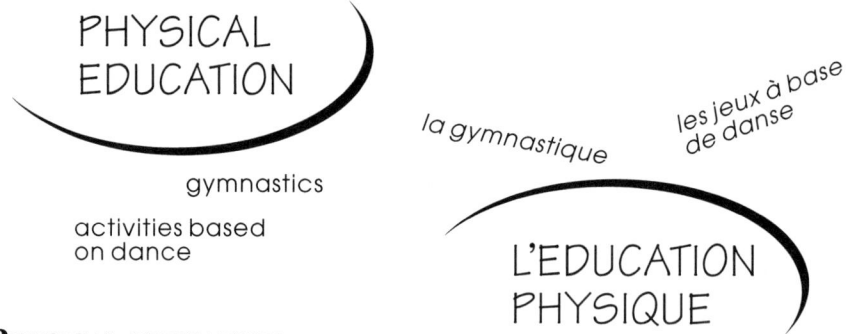

PHYSICAL EDUCATION

This unit exemplifies work drawn from the NC for England and Wales for *Key Stage 2 Physical Education (NC pages 113–118)*:

General requirements for physical education:
1. To promote physical activity . . .
2. To develop positive attitudes . . .
3. To ensure safe practice . . . respond readily to instructions
2a Gymnastic activities
a: different means of turning, rolling, swinging, jumping, climbing, balancing, travelling on hands and feet and how to adapt, practise and refine these actions, both on the floor and using apparatus
b: to emphasise changes of shape, speed and direction through gymnastic actions
3. Dance
a: to compose and control their movements by varying shape, size, direction . . .

Learning aims & objectives

Physical education

Pupils:
- increase their sense of personal confidence;
- increase mutual support;
- develop their agility and co-ordination;
- take pleasure in their physical self and in physical interaction with others.

French

Pupils hear, understand and use:
- *words for parts of the body and actions (turn, sit, roll, etc);*
- *directions;*
- *time;*
- *the language of games (sequence, instructions);*
- *prepositions (down, over, under, etc).*

52 — Young Pathfinder 7: *Making the link*

This selection of PE/games activities enables pupils to show their understanding of the foreign language by giving a physical response to the teacher's instructions, in the hall, gym, field or playground. In most of the activities a pupil could call the instructions in subsequent runs-through or in later lessons. As with PE taught through English, the activities can be taught for any length of time and in any sequence, though some warm-up activities should be used at the start of each session.

In each case, the activity is described here in English and an exemplar French version is given, though the activities lend themselves to any language. In most cases the initial teaching of language can be done by demonstration, though some phrases could usefully be pre-taught in the classroom.

JEUX D'ÉCHAUFFEMENT (WARM-UP GAMES)

Mixer / *Le jeu des aimants*

Pupils run anywhere. When the teacher calls a number, they gather in a group of that number, back to back.
Vous allez courir dans tous les sens — allez, courez — et quand je vous dirai un numéro (disons trois ou quatre, par exemple), il faudra que vous vous retrouviez en groupes de trois ou quatre, dos à dos.

Sailors / *Le jeu des marins*

The class forms a single line. When the teacher calls 'starboard', everyone runs to the right. When he or she calls 'port', they all run to the left.
Mettez-vous tous en rang, au milieu. Quand je dirai 'tribord' vous devrez tous courir vers la droite, mais quand je dirai 'babord' vous devrez courir vers la gauche.

Islands / *Le jeu des îles*

Place several different-sized hoops on the ground, forming 'islands'. The pupils run around and, on a given signal, eveyone runs to stand inside a hoop. As the game progresses, the number of hoops is reduced.
Je vais placer des cerceaux de tailles différentes par terre. Ce sont des îles. Vous allez marcher dans la pièce et quand je vous le signalerai, chacun devra courir et se mettre au milieu d'un cerceau. J'enlèverai des cerceaux au fur et à mesure. Le dernier dans un petit cerceau aura gagné.

Main activities

Break the chain / *Le jeu de la chaîne cassée*

Groups of pupils join hands, but not with the person immediately next to them. They unravel their arms to form a circle. Progressively increase the number of pupils in the group.
Vous allez vous mettre en groupes et tenir la main de quelqu'un qui n'est pas directement à côté de vous. Le but du jeu c'est de démêler les bras afin d'arriver à former un cercle.

Stubborn donkey / *Le jeu de la mule obstinée*

Pupils in pairs; one pupil in each pair on all fours and bracing him- or herself. The partner tries to push the donkey over.
Mettez-vous deux par deux. Il faut que l'un se mette à quatre pattes et refuse de bouger (c'est la mule), et que l'autre essaie de la faire se coucher par terre.

Skin the snake / *Le jeu du serpent qui pèle*

A group of about six pupils lines up one behind the other and links up by reaching backwards with one hand through their legs and taking hold of one hand of the person immediately behind. Without breaking contact the back person comes under the legs of the person in front and moves towards the front of the line. Each person follows through until the back person is at the front of the line.
Je veux que six d'entre vous se mettent en rang les uns derrière les autres. Attrapez la main de votre voisin de derrière. Le dernier devra passer sous les jambes des copains en avant sans lâcher dans main de son voisin, jusqu'à ce qu'il soit arrivé devant.

Sharks! / *Requins!*

Groups line up on a bench. The floor around the bench is shark-infested water. The pupils have to re-arrange their line according to the instructions of the teacher (i.e. tallest on right, shortest on left . . . black hair on the left, blond hair on the right, brown hair in the middle . . .) without falling into the water and being eliminated.
Mettez-vous debout sur le banc. Imaginez que le sol autour du banc est un bassin infesté de requins. Moi, je vais vous demander de changer de place selon les critères que je choisirai. Par exemple, les plus grands à droite, les moins grands à gauche . . . ceux qui ont les cheveux noirs, à droite, ceux qui ont les cheveux blonds à gauche, ceux qui ont les cheveux bruns, au milieu . . . Attention à celui qui tombe à l'eau; il sera éliminé.

Trust games / *Jeux de confiance*

Make a very simple circuit of equipment. One pupil, eyes closed, negotiates the circle under the directions of the partner. (Demonstrate with one group first, to (re)teach the phrases.)

Vous allez suivre un petit circuit (installé au préalable) les yeux fermés. Il faut éviter les obstacles en suivant les directives de votre copain.

Lap sit / *Sur mes genoux*

(This works best with a younger age group.) Pupils stand in a circle, close together, all facing in the same direction, each with their hands on the waist of the person in front. Everyone sits on the lap of the person behind.

Formez un cercle et mettez-vous debout. Regardez tous dans la même direction et mettez vos mains sur la taille du voisin de devant. Chacun doit s'asseoir sur les genoux de la personne qui est derrière.

Mime / *Jeu de mime*

Pupils sit in a circle. The teacher begins by taking an imaginary blob of clay and moulding it into a shape, starting with something straightforward such as a bird. Pupils guess what the object might be. The pupil who guesses correctly carefully takes over the clay and moulds another object. (For this activity the teacher might want to start by eliciting a list of possible items from children, then they select from the list.) Use small groups so that everyone has a turn.

Mettez-vous en cercle. Je tiens un morceau d'argile imaginaire dans mes mains et je vais lui donner une forme. A vous de deviner de quoi il s'agit. Je ferai passer délicatement le morceau d'argile à celui ou celle qui devinera. A son tour de réaliser une forme et ainsi de suite.

Wind in the willows / *Jeu du vent*

A group of eight pupils make a tight circle with their hands at chest height, palms towards the middle. One person stands in the middle, both feet together or one in front of the other to give a firm base. The person in the middle falls in any direction and the outside people push him or her around the circle.

Mettez-vous par groupes de huit et formez un cercle serré. Tendez vos bras vers l'intérieur du cercle. Un élève va se mettre au milieu, les pieds joints et le corps rigide. Il va se balancer dans une direction et vous devrez le pousser doucement dans une autre direction, comme le vent.

The monster / *Le monstre*

The object of the game is to transport a group of seven across the gym with only four anatomical points (hand, foot, etc) in contact with the ground at any one time. No props are allowed. The group must be in direct physical contact with each other as they make the crossing.

Mettez-vous par groupes de sept et serrez-vous les uns contre les autres. Le but du jeu est de traverser la salle de gym en tenant compte du fait qu'il ne peut y avoir que quatre points de contact à la fois entre le groupe et le sol. Ce point de contact peut être un pied, une main par exemple. Vous ne pouvez pas utiliser d'accessoires.

People-to-people surfing / *Le jeu du surf*

Situate the group (as many as possible) lying face down and close together side by side. A volunteer surfer lies face down at right angles on top of the 'surf'. At a given signal 'surf's up', the people under the surfer roll in a given direction, moving the surfer along the top.

Mettez-vous en groupe (aussi nombreux que possible). Allongez-vous à plat ventre sur le sol et serrez-vous les uns aux autres. Un surfeur volontaire s'allonge sur le ventre perpendiculairement aux autres; il est sur la vague. Au signal 'surfez!', les élèves sous le surfeur devront rouler dans la direction indiquée. Il doit se transporter ainsi à l'autre bout de la vague.

Brroom-brroom (for infants) / *Vroum*

The pupils sit in a large circle. Imagine 'brroom-brroom' as the sound of a Formula 1 racing car. Start by saying 'brroom-brroom' and turn your head to the right or left of the circle. The person on that side passes the word to the next person and around the circle. If you wish to change the direction of the word, you must say 'eeeek'. The word 'eeeek' makes the car stop and change direction. (It is best if you restrict the use of the word 'eeeek' to one or two pupils.)

Tout le monde s'assied et forme un grand cercle. 'Vroum', c'est le bruit d'une voiture de course, un bolide Formule 1. Je vais dire 'vroum' et tourner la tête à gauche ou à droite. La personne qui se trouve de ce côté doit faire passer le mot à la prochaine et ainsi de suite. On peut changer direction si on dit 'hiiiii'. Dans ce cas, la voiture s'arrête et repart de l'autre côté.

Tortoises / *Le jeu des tortues*

A group of pupils gather under a mat and try to move over a given course (teacher gives directions) as a tortoise.
Mettez-vous en groupe à quatre pattes sous un tapis et essayez d'avancer comme une tortue tout en suivant les directions que je vous indiquerai.

Clock and compass / *La montre et la boussole*

Pupils lie face-up on the ground, all heads pointing the same way. The teacher calls a time and the children swing their bodies round to point to that hour (change to points of the compass).
Allongez-vous sur le sol; et imaginez que votre tête est une aiguille. On va dire que la porte représente midi (le nord). Je vais vous dire une heure (une direction); le plus rapidement possible, vous allez vous tourner dans ce sens.

PARACHUTE GAMES

Waves / *Le jeu des vagues*

Pupils kneel down and hold the parachute, making 'waves' with it. Allow two or three children to walk or run in the waves, which get rougher/calmer at your command.
Mettez-vous à genoux en cercle; tenez le parachute. Faites-lui faire des vagues. Deux ou trois d'entre vous . . . voyons, A, B et C . . . vont monter dessus et essayer de marcher ou courir dans la mer. Mais attention, la tempête peut se lever à tout instant (tempête! . . . mer calme! . . .).

Mushroom / *Le jeu du champignon*

The pupils position themselves around the parachute. On a given signal they simultaneously lift the parachute to form a mushroom. While the 'chute is raised, the teacher calls to a group of pupils to let go and run underneath to the other side, e.g. children wearing white shorts, grey socks, with long hair, etc.
Mettez-vous debout, en cercle, et tenez le parachute. A mon signal, vous allez le soulever et lui donner la forme d'un champignon. A ce moment-là je vais en désigner quelques uns (tous ceux qui portent un short blanc/des chaussettes grises/ceux qui ont des cheveux longs, etc) et ils devront courir sous le champignon jusqu'à l'autre côté du cercle.

Conclusion

Chapters 1 to 5 offer a compendium of activities which can also be used by teachers whose own command of the foreign language may not be extensive. The activities have been tried and tested, are engaging and communicative, and should help teachers to introduce the foreign language even to children in the earlier primary years.

Teachers whose language competence and confidence improve — either through use in the classroom or through further language training — or who are already confident and fluent may feel able to go on to linguistically more demanding activities with pupils in the later primary years.

The activities in Chapter 6 are examples of what can be done by a teacher with some foreign language proficiency who wants to teach 'unbroken' lessons in French, based on purposeful familiar activities which pupils will have met in other subjects. This chapter is not intended to be a completed scheme of work. It provides some models which teachers can use in order to devise their own foreign language material (not necessarily French), based on activities which are already in their schemes of work for topics and subject of the curriculum for the Key Stage 2 age group.

The structure of the activities given here suggests how careful planning of the learning objectives, language objectives, vocabulary and cross-referencing to the National Curriculum can help to successfully re-teach some mother tongue activities as activities in the foreign language.

Together, all the activities suggested in this Young Pathfinder illustrate how, from an early start of introducing a small amount of simple language to the progressively more challenging language, it is possible to integrate the foreign language into the 'regular' curriculum and, in the process, re-enforce learner skills which have been developed in other subjects.

Useful sources

Advice for schools (SOEID, 1995; 1996; 1997)

Berwick G and P Horsfall, *Making effective use of the dictionary*, (CILT, 1996)

Martin C with C Cheater, *Let's join in! Rhymes, poems and songs* (CILT, 1998)

Martin C, *Games and fun activities* (CILT, 1995)

Modern languages in the primary school (SOEID/SCOPE/SITC, 1994). 3 CD-i and viewing guide

Modern languages in the primary school (SOEID/SCET, 1993). The national training programmes in French, German, Italian and Spanish

Modern languages in the primary school (SOEID/SCOPE, 1993). 3 videos and viewing guide

Satchell P, *Keep talking: teaching in the target language* (CILT, 1997)

Satchell P and J de Silva, *Catching them young* (CILT, 1995)

Skarbek C, *First steps to reading and writing* (CILT, 1998)

Staff development French (SOEID/SITC, 1997). CD-i

Tierney D and P Dobson, *Are you sitting comfortably? Telling stories to young language learners* (CILT, 1995)